Biblical Wisdom on Wealth:

Unveiling the Secrets of Prosperity

Copyright © 2023 by Maxwell Angelou
All rights reserved. No part of this publication may be reproduced, distributed, or transmitted in any form or by any means, including photocopying, recording, or other electronic or mechanical methods, without the prior written permission of the publisher, except as permitted by U.S. copyright law. For permission requests, contact
Maxwell Angelou.
Book Cover by Maxwell

01 edition 2024

Table of Contents

Introduction

1.1 Purpose of the Book **6**

1.2 Understanding the Biblical Perspective on Wealth **9**

Chapter One: The Blessings of Diligence

1.1 Proverbs 10:4 - "Lazy hands make for poverty, but diligent hands bring wealth." **12**

1.2 Exploring the Connection Between Hard Work and Prosperity **14**

Chapter Two: God's Provision

2.1 Matthew 6:26 - "Look at the birds of the air; they do not sow or reap or store away in barns, and yet your heavenly Father feeds them. Are you not much more valuable than they?" **18**

2.2 Trusting in God's Provision for Financial Stability **21**

Chapter Three: Stewardship and Generosity

3.1 Proverbs 3:9-10 - "Honor the Lord with your wealth, with the firstfruits of all your crops; then your barns will be filled to overflowing, and your vats will brim over with new wine." **26**

3.2 Exploring the Concept of Tithing and Generosity in Biblical Context **31**

Chapter Four: The Dangers of Love for Money

4.1 1 Timothy 6:10 - "For the love of money is a root of all kinds of evil. Some people, eager for money, have wandered from the faith and pierced themselves with many griefs." **34**

4.2 Understanding the Pitfalls of an Unhealthy Attachment to Wealth **39**

Chapter Five: Contentment and Gratitude

5.1 Philippians 4:11-13 - "I am not saying this because I am in need, for I have learned to be content whatever the circumstances. I know what it is to be in need, and I know what it is to have plenty. I have learned the secret of being content in any and every situation, whether well fed or hungry, whether living in plenty or in want." **44**

5.2 Finding True Riches in Contentment and Gratitude **50**

Chapter Six: Seeking God's Kingdom First

6.1 Matthew 6:33 - "But seek first his kingdom and his righteousness, and all these things will be given to you as well." **52**

6.2 Prioritizing Spiritual Wealth and Trusting God's Provision **57**

Chapter Seven: Investing in Eternal Treasures

7.1 Matthew 6:19-21 - "Do not store up for yourselves treasures on earth, where moths and vermin destroy, and where thieves break in and steal. But store up for yourselves treasures in heaven, where moths and vermin do not destroy, and where thieves do not break in and steal. For where your treasure is, there your heart will be also." **65**

7.2 Understanding the Impermanence of Earthly Wealth and the Importance of Eternal Investments **68**

Conclusion

8.1 Recapitulation of Key Biblical Principles on Money and Wealth .. **75**

8.2 Encouragement for a Balanced and God-Centered Approach to Finances .**78**

Introduction

In a world shaped by the pursuit of prosperity and financial success, the Bible stands as an enduring source of wisdom, offering insights into the intricate relationship between humanity and wealth. "Biblical Wisdom on Wealth: Unveiling the Secrets of Prosperity" seeks to unravel the age-old scriptures that guide us in understanding money and riches from a divine perspective.

The purpose of this book is to explore the teachings of the Bible concerning wealth, prosperity, and the responsible stewardship of resources. As we delve into the scriptures, we aim to provide a comprehensive and insightful look at how the biblical principles can shape our attitudes and actions toward money.

Throughout the pages that follow, we will journey through various passages that address the blessings of diligence, God's provision, stewardship, generosity, the dangers of love for money, contentment, seeking God's kingdom first, and the eternal perspective on wealth. Each chapter will focus on a specific aspect of the biblical teachings, offering a blend of scriptural insight and practical application.

It is our hope that this exploration will lead you to a deeper understanding of the spiritual dimensions of wealth, encouraging you to align your financial practices with the timeless principles found in the Word of God. As we embark on this journey together, may we discover the secrets of true prosperity and find fulfillment in a life that reflects the divine wisdom on money and wealth.

1.1 Purpose of the Book

The purpose of "Biblical Wisdom on Wealth: Unveiling the Secrets of Prosperity" goes beyond a mere exploration of scriptures related to money; it seeks to provide readers with a transformative understanding of wealth from a biblical standpoint. The primary objectives of this book are as follows:

Spiritual Enlightenment

The book aims to enlighten readers on the spiritual dimensions of wealth, emphasizing the profound connection between one's faith and financial practices. By delving into the scriptures, it aspires to reveal the underlying principles that can guide individuals towards a more purposeful and God-centered approach to managing resources.

Practical Application

While rooted in biblical teachings, the book doesn't remain confined to theoretical discussions. It endeavors to bridge the gap between scripture and everyday life by offering practical insights and applications. Readers will find guidance on how to integrate biblical principles into their financial decisions, fostering a sense of stewardship and responsibility.

Holistic Approach

Recognizing that wealth encompasses more than just material possessions, the book takes a holistic approach. It addresses aspects such as contentment, generosity, and the pursuit of eternal treasures, encouraging readers to view wealth not merely as a means of personal gain but as a tool for positive impact and spiritual growth.

Navigating Challenges

The exploration of scriptures about the dangers of love for money serves as a cautionary guide. The book aims to equip readers with the knowledge and awareness necessary to navigate the potential pitfalls associated with wealth, promoting a balanced and ethical approach to financial success.

Encouragement and Empowerment

Through the biblical narratives and teachings, the book seeks to inspire and empower readers. By understanding the promises, principles, and warnings found in the Bible, individuals can embark on a journey of financial well-being with confidence, trust, and a sense of purpose.

Cultivating a Heart of Gratitude

One of the underlying purposes of this book is to foster a mindset of gratitude and contentment. By exploring the biblical passages that speak to being content in all circumstances, readers are encouraged to appreciate the blessings they have, whether abundant or meager. Gratitude becomes a powerful force in reshaping perspectives on wealth and material possessions.

Promoting Generosity and Social Responsibility

Building on the biblical principle of generosity, this book encourages readers to view their wealth as a means to bless others. Understanding the concept of stewardship involves recognizing the responsibility to share resources with those in need. The book provides insights into how generosity and social responsibility can be integrated into one's financial practices, contributing to a more compassionate and just society.

Addressing Cultural and Societal Influences

Recognizing the impact of cultural and societal norms on attitudes towards wealth, this book aims to challenge and reshape perspectives. By juxtaposing contemporary financial ideologies with biblical truths, readers are invited to critically evaluate societal expectations and norms, guiding them towards a worldview aligned with divine principles.

Navigating Economic Challenges

In acknowledging the economic challenges that individuals and communities face, the book aims to provide hope and resilience through the lens of biblical teachings. By offering a perspective that transcends economic hardships, readers can find strength, perseverance, and innovative solutions rooted in the wisdom of scripture.

Fostering Financial Well-Being

Ultimately, the purpose of this book is to contribute to the holistic well-being of individuals. By combining spiritual insights with practical financial wisdom, readers are empowered to make informed and responsible decisions that lead to financial stability and prosperity. The book seeks to be a guiding light on the journey to financial well-being, acknowledging that true wealth encompasses not only financial success but also emotional, relational, and spiritual flourishing.

As readers embark on this exploration of biblical wisdom on wealth, the overarching goal is to facilitate a paradigm shift that transcends the conventional understanding of prosperity, inviting individuals to embrace a richer, more meaningful, and spiritually grounded life.

1.2 Understanding the Biblical Perspective on Wealth:

To truly grasp the essence of the biblical teachings on wealth, it is essential to delve into the overarching perspective the Bible presents on this multifaceted subject. The biblical perspective on wealth is characterized by a profound integration of faith, values, and practical living. Here are key facets that contribute to a comprehensive understanding:

Stewardship and Ownership: The Bible emphasizes the concept of stewardship, asserting that everything belongs to God, and humanity is entrusted with the responsibility of managing these resources. Wealth, therefore, is seen as a divine gift to be used wisely and responsibly, acknowledging God as the ultimate owner.

God's Provision and Blessings: Numerous scriptures highlight the idea that God is the ultimate provider of wealth. From the abundance of crops to the skills and abilities that lead to prosperity, the Bible underscores the notion that all good things come from God's gracious hand. Understanding wealth in this context fosters a spirit of gratitude and humility.

Balancing Material and Spiritual Priorities: The biblical perspective on wealth urges individuals to seek first the kingdom of God. This involves prioritizing spiritual well-being and aligning one's pursuits with God's purposes. The emphasis is on maintaining a balance between the pursuit of material prosperity and the higher calling of spiritual growth and obedience.

Generosity and Compassion: Generosity is a recurring theme in the Bible, emphasizing the responsibility to share one's wealth with others, particularly those in need. The act of giving is viewed as an expression of love and compassion, reflecting the generous nature of God. Through acts of kindness and charity, individuals participate in God's redemptive work in the world.

Contentment and Detachment: Biblical teachings caution against the love

Of money and encourage contentment in all circumstances. This perspective emphasizes the transitory nature of material possessions and the importance of finding satisfaction in God rather than in wealth. Detachment from an excessive attachment to worldly riches fosters spiritual freedom and true contentment.

Eternal Perspective: The Bible presents an eternal perspective on wealth, urging believers to invest in treasures that transcend the temporal. The impermanence of earthly possessions is contrasted with the enduring value of heavenly treasures. This perspective prompts individuals to consider the eternal impact of their financial decisions and investments.

Cautions and Warnings: While acknowledging the potential benefits of wealth, the Bible also offers warnings about the dangers of an unhealthy relationship with money. Scriptures caution against the love of money, greed, and the pursuit of wealth at the expense of one's faith and integrity. These warnings serve as a guide to navigate the potential pitfalls associated with financial success.

Understanding the biblical perspective on wealth involves embracing a holistic worldview that integrates spiritual principles into financial decisions. It invites individuals to view wealth not as an end in itself but as a means to glorify God, contribute to the well-being of others, and participate in the unfolding of God's redemptive plan for humanity. As we explore the scriptures in the following chapters, we will delve deeper into these foundational principles, unraveling the timeless wisdom that shapes the biblical perspective on wealth.

- CHAPTER 1 -

The Blessings of Diligence

1.1 Proverbs 10:4 - "Lazy hands make for poverty, but diligent hands bring wealth."

This proverb encapsulates a timeless truth about the correlation between industriousness and financial well-being. The Book of Proverbs, known for its practical wisdom, provides valuable insights into the virtues of diligence and the consequences of idleness.

Interpreting Proverbs 10:4

Lazy Hands and Poverty: The term "lazy hands" implies a lack of diligence, initiative, and industrious effort. Proverbs asserts that such an attitude leads to poverty. Laziness, in this context, is not merely physical but extends to a mindset that avoids responsibility, work, and the disciplined pursuit of goals.

Diligent Hands and Wealth: On the contrary, "diligent hands" symbolize a proactive and hardworking approach to life. Diligence involves consistent effort, perseverance, and a commitment to excellence. According to this proverb, such diligence is rewarded with wealth. It suggests that a diligent person is more likely to experience financial prosperity and success.

Practical Application:

Work Ethic: The proverb encourages a strong work ethic, emphasizing the importance of putting in the effort and energy required for success. Diligent hands are not passive but actively engaged in productive activities.

Discipline and Consistency: Diligence involves discipline and consistency in one's actions. It implies setting goals, staying focused, and consistently working towards achieving them. This disciplined approach is portrayed as a pathway to financial abundance.

Avoidance of Procrastination: Laziness often manifests in procrastination and avoidance of responsibilities. The proverb challenges individuals to overcome procrastination and embrace a proactive mindset that tackles tasks and challenges promptly.

Understanding Wealth in a Holistic Sense: While the proverb highlights the correlation between diligence and wealth, it is essential to understand wealth in a holistic sense. True wealth encompasses not only financial prosperity but also spiritual, emotional, and relational well-being.

Spiritual Insight:

The biblical perspective on diligence goes beyond material success; it is deeply rooted in spiritual principles. The Bible encourages believers to work diligently, not just for personal gain but as an expression of stewardship and service to God and others.

As we explore the blessings of diligence, let us reflect on how the principles outlined in Proverbs 10:4 can guide us in cultivating a work ethic that aligns with God's design for a purposeful and prosperous life. In the following sections, we will continue to uncover additional scriptures that provide further insights into the biblical teachings on wealth and the virtues that lead to prosperity.

1.2 Exploring the Connection Between Hard Work and Prosperity

Building upon the foundation laid by Proverbs 10:4, which highlights the relationship between diligence and wealth, we delve deeper into the biblical teachings that underscore the connection between hard work and prosperity. This chapter seeks to explore additional scriptures that offer profound insights into the spiritual and practical aspects of diligence and its impact on one's financial well-being.

Ecclesiastes 9:10 - "Whatever your hand finds to do, do it with all your might, for in the realm of the dead, where you are going, there is neither working nor planning nor knowledge nor wisdom."

This verse from Ecclesiastes emphasizes the urgency and wholeheartedness with which one should approach their work. It acknowledges the finite nature of life and urges individuals to engage in their endeavors with dedication and excellence. By doing so, one not only contributes to their prosperity but also honors God through the responsible use of their abilities.

Colossians 3:23-24 - "Whatever you do, work at it with all your heart, as working for the Lord, not for human masters, since you know that you will receive an inheritance from the Lord as a reward. It is the Lord Christ you are serving."

In the New Testament, Colossians reinforces the concept of wholehearted work, emphasizing that our efforts are ultimately in service to God. This perspective transforms mundane tasks into opportunities for spiritual devotion, contributing to a sense of purpose and fulfillment in both our earthly endeavors and eternal rewards.

Proverbs 13:4 - "A sluggard's appetite is never filled, but the desires of the diligent are fully satisfied."

This proverb provides a contrast between the lazy and the diligent. It suggests that a diligent person, by consistently applying effort and diligence, experiences a fulfillment of desires. Diligence not only leads to prosperity but also satisfies the deeper longings of the heart, fostering contentment and a sense of achievement.

Reflection and Application:

Integrity in Work: The biblical teachings encourage not only hard work but also the importance of maintaining integrity in our endeavors. Diligence is not solely about achieving success but also about conducting oneself with honesty and ethical principles.

Dedication to God: Both Ecclesiastes and Colossians highlight the spiritual significance of work. When approached with dedication and a heart for service to God, our work becomes a form of worship, contributing to a holistic understanding of prosperity that encompasses the spiritual realm.

Fulfillment through Diligence: Proverbs 13:4 prompts reflection on the nature of desires and contentment. Diligence, as portrayed in this proverb, brings about a unique sense of satisfaction, transcending mere material accumulation and addressing the deeper aspects of human fulfillment.

Balancing Work and Rest: While diligence is vital, the Bible also emphasizes the importance of rest. A balanced approach to work includes recognizing the need for Sabbath rest and trusting God's provision.

Psalm 1:3 - "That person is like a tree planted by streams of water, which yields its fruit in season and whose leaf does not wither—whatever they do prospers."

Psalm 1 beautifully illustrates the imagery of a flourishing tree as a metaphor for a person who delights in God's Word. Such an individual, grounded in spiritual principles, is likened to a tree planted by streams of water—

receiving nourishment and strength. The verse emphasizes that whatever this person does prospers, underscoring the interconnectedness of spiritual well-being and the prosperity that flows from a life aligned with God's guidance.

Proverbs 22:29 - "Do you see someone skilled in their work? They will serve before kings; they will not serve before officials of low rank."

This proverb highlights the link between excellence in one's craft and the opportunities for success it can bring. Those who diligently hone their skills and work with excellence are positioned for advancement and influence. The emphasis here is on continuous improvement and mastery in one's field, demonstrating that prosperity often follows those who invest in developing their abilities.

2 Thessalonians 3:10b - "If anyone is not willing to work, let him not eat."

While the Bible extols the virtues of hard work, it also addresses the responsibility to work for sustenance. This verse from 2 Thessalonians reinforces the biblical ethic of diligence and self-sufficiency. It encourages a balanced perspective, emphasizing the importance of personal effort in meeting one's basic needs and contributing to the well-being of the community.

Reflection and Application:

Alignment with God's Word: Psalm 1 provides a profound insight into the connection between a life rooted in God's Word and overall prosperity. As we align our actions with biblical principles, we position ourselves to experience true abundance, extending beyond material wealth to encompass spiritual and emotional well-being.

Excellence and Influence: Proverbs 22:29 underscores the impact of skill and excellence in one's work. Striving for mastery and delivering quality in our endeavors not only leads to personal success but also positions us to serve in influential capacities, contributing positively to the community and society at large.

Balancing Work and Basic Needs: 2 Thessalonians 3:10b emphasizes the biblical principle of self-sufficiency and the importance of work in meeting basic needs. This aligns with the broader biblical narrative of responsibility, diligence, and contributing positively to the welfare of oneself and others.

Holistic Prosperity: Collectively, these verses paint a picture of holistic prosperity—one that encompasses spiritual vitality, professional success, and responsible self-sufficiency. It challenges us to view prosperity not as a narrow pursuit of wealth but as a multidimensional concept that reflects a life lived in accordance with God's design.

As we continue our exploration of biblical wisdom on wealth, these scriptures guide us in understanding the intricate relationship between hard work, spiritual alignment, and the diverse dimensions of prosperity. May these insights inspire us to approach our work with dedication, excellence, and a heart attuned to God's purposes.

- CHAPTER 2 -

God's Provision

2.1 Matthew 6:26 - "Look at the birds of the air; they do not sow or reap or store away in barns, and yet your heavenly Father feeds them. Are you not much more valuable than they?"

This verse, spoken by Jesus in the Sermon on the Mount, serves as a powerful reminder of God's provision and care for His creation. By directing our attention to the birds of the air, Jesus invites us to contemplate the simplicity of their lives and how God ensures their sustenance. In doing so, he emphasizes a profound truth about God's care for His children.

Interpreting Matthew 6:26

Observing God's Creation: Jesus encourages his followers to look at the birds as a source of instruction and inspiration. Birds, without engaging in the toil of farming or storing provisions, receive their daily sustenance directly from the hand of God.

Comparing Human Value: The rhetorical question Jesus poses—"Are you not much more valuable than they?"—challenges his listeners to recognize their inherent worth in God's eyes. If God provides for the needs of birds, how much more will He care for and provide for those created in His image?

Practical Application:

Trusting in God's Provision: This verse calls believers to trust in God's provision with the confidence that, as valued children of God, their needs will be met. It encourages a mindset of reliance on God's faithfulness rather than excessive worry about material concerns.

Recognizing God's Love: The comparison between the care God provides for birds and His care for humanity reinforces the concept of God's boundless love. It emphasizes that God's love extends to the practical aspects of our lives, including our daily needs for sustenance.

Fostering Contentment: By acknowledging God's provision for even the smallest creatures, the verse promotes contentment. It encourages believers to find peace in the assurance that God, who cares for birds, will undoubtedly care for His cherished human creation.

Spiritual Insight:

This scripture holds spiritual significance beyond the practical aspect of provision. It speaks to the character of God as a loving and attentive Father who not only meets our physical needs but also values our well-being. It encourages believers to approach life with confidence, knowing that they are under the watchful care of a compassionate God.

Reflection and Application:

Cultivating Trust: Matthew 6:26 challenges us to cultivate trust in God's character. When faced with uncertainties or anxieties, we can draw strength from the assurance that God, who cares for the birds of the air, is intimately concerned with our lives.

Expressing Gratitude: Contemplating God's provision for the birds prompts a spirit of gratitude. Recognizing the abundance of God's blessings, both seen and unseen, encourages believers to approach life with a heart overflowing with thanksgiving.

Reevaluating Priorities: The verse encourages a reevaluation of priorities. Rather than obsessing over worldly concerns, believers are prompted to focus on their relationship with God and trust in His divine provision.

Encouraging Generosity: Matthew 6:26, while highlighting God's provision, also indirectly encourages a spirit of generosity. If God, in His abundance, cares for the needs of even the smallest creatures, how much more should believers be willing to share their resources with others in need? This verse challenges us to consider the divine example of provision as a call to generosity and compassion towards our fellow human beings.

Emphasizing the Temporary Nature of Wealth: By drawing attention to the birds' lack of agricultural activity and storage practices, Jesus implies the temporary nature of material wealth. This verse serves as a reminder that while financial planning and responsible stewardship are important, ultimate reliance should be on God's enduring provision rather than accumulating possessions as a primary source of security.

Holistic Reflection and Application:

Balancing Planning and Trust: Matthew 6:26 encourages a balance between prudent planning and unwavering trust in God. While responsible financial stewardship is commendable, the verse cautions against excessive worry and emphasizes the importance of trusting in God's provision.

Compassionate Living: Understanding God's care for the birds prompts believers to adopt a compassionate and empathetic lifestyle. It encourages us to extend care and support to those around us, recognizing that our Heavenly Father's love encompasses not only our needs but also our capacity to love others.

Building a Foundation of Faith: This scripture invites believers to build their lives on a foundation of faith. By trusting in God's provision and acknowledging His care for all aspects of life, individuals can cultivate a resilient faith that sustains them through various circumstances, including financial challenges.

Seeking God's Kingdom First: As part of the broader context of the Sermon on the Mount, this verse aligns with Jesus' teaching in Matthew 6:33 – "But seek first his kingdom and his righteousness, and all these things will be given to you as well." It emphasizes the priority of seeking God's kingdom and righteousness over preoccupation with material concerns, promising that God's provision follows a heart dedicated to His purposes.

Incorporating these insights into our understanding of wealth, provision, and generosity, Matthew 6:26 encourages a holistic approach to life—one that recognizes the interconnectedness of spiritual principles and practical living. As we continue our exploration, let us carry these lessons into our daily endeavors, trusting in God's provision while actively engaging in a life that reflects His love and generosity.

2.2 Trusting in God's Provision for Financial Stability

Building on the foundation of Matthew 6:26, this section delves deeper into the theme of trusting in God's provision for financial stability. The scripture serves as a cornerstone for understanding how reliance on God can bring stability to our financial lives, offering a counter-cultural perspective in a world often marked by anxiety and self-reliance.

Psalm 37:25 - "I was young and now I am old, yet I have never seen the righteous forsaken or their children begging bread."

The Psalmist reflects on a lifetime of experience and testifies to the faithfulness of God. The assertion that the righteous are never forsaken underscores the idea that those who align their lives with God's ways can trust in His continual provision. The imagery of children not begging for bread highlights God's enduring care for generations.

Philippians 4:19 - "And my God will meet all your needs according to the riches of his glory in Christ Jesus."

The apostle Paul, writing to the Philippians, expresses confidence in God's ability to meet all needs. This verse emphasizes the comprehensive nature of God's provision, assuring believers that every aspect of their lives, including financial needs, is within the scope of God's care.

Proverbs 3:5-6 - "Trust in the Lord with all your heart and lean not on your own understanding; in all your ways submit to him, and he will make your paths straight."

Proverbs 3:5-6 offers a timeless admonition to trust in the Lord wholeheartedly. The promise of God directing one's paths implies not only guidance but also a divine orchestration that includes provision. Trusting God with our financial stability involves relinquishing self-reliance and embracing a posture of dependence on His wisdom and care.

Practical Application:

Cultivating Trust through Faithfulness: Psalm 37:25 encourages believers to cultivate a lifestyle of faithfulness to God. Trusting in God's provision for financial stability is intertwined with a commitment to live in alignment with His principles and seek His righteousness.

Embracing Contentment: Philippians 4:19 emphasizes the sufficiency of God's provision according to His riches. This truth invites believers to embrace contentment, recognizing that God's provision is not just about meeting needs but about fulfilling them in a way that reflects His abundance.

Seeking Guidance in Decision-Making: Proverbs 3:5-6 challenges individuals to submit all aspects of their lives, including financial matters, to God. This involves seeking His guidance in decision-making, acknowledging that true financial stability is found in following the paths God directs.

Spiritual Insight:

The scriptures presented emphasize not only the provision itself but also the relational aspect of trusting in God. The foundation of trust is built on a personal relationship with a faithful and loving God, and financial stability is a natural outgrowth of that trust.

Reflection and Application:

Assessing Our Trust in God: Reflecting on these scriptures prompts believers to assess the depth of their trust in God, especially concerning financial matters. It encourages an evaluation of whether trust is rooted in personal understanding or in surrendering to God's wisdom.

Aligning Priorities with God's Kingdom: Trusting in God's provision for financial stability requires a deliberate alignment of priorities with God's kingdom. This involves seeking first His righteousness, as Jesus teaches in Matthew 6:33, and trusting that all necessary provisions will follow.

Responding to Challenges with Faith: As life presents financial challenges, these scriptures provide a foundation for responding with faith rather than fear. The testimonies of the Psalmist and the apostle Paul assure believers that God's provision is steadfast and faithful.

As we explore the concept of trusting in God's provision for financial stability, let these scriptures guide us in cultivating a resilient trust in God's faithfulness, acknowledging His role as the ultimate provider in our lives. May this trust become a source of peace, contentment, and steadfastness in the face of financial uncertainties.

Generosity in Abundance: Trusting in God's provision extends beyond personal financial stability; it also opens the door to a spirit of generosity. When believers trust that God will meet their needs, it frees them to share abundantly with others. This generosity, rooted in the confidence of God's ongoing provision, becomes a testimony of faith and a means through which God's blessings flow.

Understanding God's Timing: The journey of trusting in God's provision often involves an understanding of His timing. Psalm 37:25, reflecting on a lifetime, suggests that God's provision may not always align with immediate expectations. Trusting in God's timing fosters patience and a deeper reliance on His wisdom and perfect plan.

Ecclesiastes 5:19 - "Moreover, when God gives someone wealth and possessions, and the ability to enjoy them, to accept their lot and be happy in their toil—this is a gift of God."

Ecclesiastes offers a perspective on wealth that goes beyond mere provision. The passage highlights the enjoyment of wealth as a gift from God. Trusting in God's provision involves recognizing not only the necessity of provision but also the gratitude and contentment that come with His blessings.

James 1:17 - "Every good and perfect gift is from above, coming down

from the Father of the heavenly lights, who does not change like shifting shadows."

James reinforces the idea that all good things, including financial stability, are gifts from God. Trusting in His unchanging nature brings assurance that His provision remains constant even in the midst of life's uncertainties.

Practical Application:

Cultivating a Heart of Gratitude: Ecclesiastes 5:19 and James 1:17 inspire believers to cultivate a heart of gratitude. Recognizing God's provision as a gift prompts an attitude of thankfulness, fostering contentment and joy in the midst of financial circumstances.

Balancing Enjoyment and Stewardship: Ecclesiastes encourages believers not only to receive God's gifts but also to enjoy them responsibly. Trusting in God's provision involves striking a balance between enjoying the blessings He provides and stewarding them wisely for His purposes.

Steadfastness Amid Change: James 1:17 anchors believers in the unchanging nature of God. In a world marked by shifting circumstances, trusting in God's provision provides a stable foundation, fostering steadfastness and resilience in the face of life's fluctuations.

Spiritual Insight:

These scriptures emphasize that trusting in God's provision goes beyond a transactional relationship—it is about recognizing God as the ultimate source of all blessings and acknowledging His sovereign control over every aspect of our lives.

Reflection and Application:

Cultivating a Lifestyle of Gratitude: Reflecting on Ecclesiastes 5:19 and James 1:17 challenges believers to cultivate a lifestyle of gratitude, acknowledging God's provision as gifts to be cherished. This mindset transforms the way we view our financial circumstances.

Practicing Enjoyment with Responsibility: Ecclesiastes encourages believers to enjoy God's gifts while remaining responsible stewards. This prompts a reflection on how one can strike a balance between enjoying financial blessings and stewarding them wisely for God's purposes.

Anchoring Trust in God's Unchanging Nature: James 1:17 serves as a reminder to anchor our trust in the unchanging character of God. Trusting in His provision involves relying on His consistent and faithful nature, even when external circumstances may shift.

Responding to God's Provision with Generosity: The understanding that God's provision is a gift invites believers to respond with generosity. As financial stability is viewed as a manifestation of God's grace, it prompts a willingness to share those blessings with others.

As we deepen our exploration of trusting in God's provision for financial stability, let these scriptures guide us in cultivating gratitude, responsibility, and generosity. May our trust in God's provision not only bring personal peace but also radiate outward, impacting the lives of others as a testament to God's faithfulness.

- CHAPTER 3 -

Stewardship and Generosity

3.1 Proverbs 3:9-10 - *"Honor the Lord with your wealth, with the firstfruits of all your crops; then your barns will be filled to overflowing, and your vats will brim over with new wine."*

Proverbs 3:9-10 presents a profound principle of honoring God with one's wealth, recognizing His role as the ultimate source of prosperity. This passage encourages believers to prioritize God in their financial stewardship and promises abundant blessings in return.

Interpreting Proverbs 3:9-10

Honoring God with the Firstfruits: The command to offer the "firstfruits" signifies a gesture of priority and reverence. In ancient agricultural practices, the first portion of the harvest represented the best and most valuable, signifying an acknowledgment that all blessings come from God.

Overflowing Blessings: The promise attached to honoring God with one's wealth is abundant blessings. The imagery of barns filled to overflowing and vats brimming over with new wine illustrates God's desire to pour out prosperity upon those who prioritize Him in their financial affairs.

Practical Application:

Prioritizing God in Finances: Proverbs 3:9-10 challenges believers to intentionally prioritize God with their finances. It involves acknowledging His ownership of all resources and expressing gratitude by giving the first and best portion back to Him.

Cultivating a Heart of Generosity: Beyond a mere financial transaction, honoring God with wealth involves cultivating a heart of generosity. It reflects an understanding that God's blessings are meant to be shared, contributing to the well-being of others and furthering God's kingdom.

Trusting in God's Provision: The promise of overflowing blessings in return encourages believers to trust in God's provision. This trust involves recognizing that, by honoring God with their wealth, individuals open themselves to the limitless abundance that flows from His gracious hand.

Spiritual Insight:

Proverbs 3:9-10 provides spiritual insight into the symbiotic relationship between honoring God with wealth and receiving His abundant blessings. It underscores the principle that generous giving is not a loss but an investment in God's economy, where generosity begets overflow.

Reflection and Application:

Reflecting on Priorities: Proverbs 3:9-10 prompts believers to reflect on their priorities in financial matters. It challenges the notion that financial decisions are solely personal and encourages a shift toward recognizing God's rightful place in the allocation of resources.

Generosity as an Expression of Faith: Honoring God with wealth becomes an expression of faith. Reflecting on this passage encourages believers to view financial decisions not only through the lens of stewardship but also as an opportunity to express trust in God's promises.

Gratitude in Financial Stewardship: The act of giving the firstfruits expresses gratitude. Believers are encouraged to approach financial stewardship with a heart of thanksgiving, recognizing that every blessing, including financial resources, is a gift from God.

Anticipating Overflow: Proverbs 3:9-10 invites believers to anticipate and trust in the overflow of blessings that result from honoring God with their wealth. This perspective transforms the act of giving into a hopeful and expectant expression of faith in God's faithfulness.

Understanding the Principle of Firstfruits: The concept of offering firstfruits goes beyond a mere financial transaction; it symbolizes an acknowledgment of God's sovereignty and provision. By giving the first and best portion to God, individuals demonstrate their dependence on Him for sustenance and express gratitude for His continuous blessings.

Cultivating a Habit of Gratitude: Honoring God with wealth is intricately tied to cultivating a habit of gratitude. The act of giving firstfruits is an intentional practice that prompts believers to regularly reflect on the abundance of God's provision and respond with a thankful heart.

Malachi 3:10 - "Bring the whole tithe into the storehouse, that there may be food in my house. Test me in this," says the Lord Almighty, "and see if I will not throw open the floodgates of heaven and pour out so much blessing that there will not be room enough to store it."

This verse from Malachi echoes the theme of honoring God with one's wealth, specifically through the practice of tithing. The imagery of opening the floodgates of heaven portrays a divine response to faithful stewardship, emphasizing God's willingness to pour out blessings in abundance when His people honor Him with their resources.

Luke 6:38 - "Give, and it will be given to you. A good measure, pressed down, shaken together and running over, will be poured into your lap. For with the measure you use, it will be measured to you."

Jesus, in Luke 6:38, reinforces the principle of generosity and reciprocity. The metaphor of a good measure, pressed down, shaken together, and running over illustrates the abundance that results from a generous and giving heart. This verse emphasizes the interconnectedness of giving and receiving in God's economy.

Practical Application:

Faithfulness in Tithing: Malachi 3:10 encourages believers to bring the whole tithe into God's storehouse. Tithing is a tangible expression of faithfulness in honoring God with the firstfruits of one's income, acknowledging His ownership and provision.

Testing God's Faithfulness: Malachi presents a unique invitation to test God's faithfulness in financial matters. Believers are encouraged to step out in faith, trusting that as they honor God with their resources, He will respond with an overflow of blessings that surpass human comprehension.

Reciprocity in Giving: Luke 6:38 introduces the principle of reciprocity in giving. The imagery of a generous measure being poured back into one's lap emphasizes that the blessings resulting from giving are not merely equal but exceed the measure of one's generosity.

Spiritual Insight:

These scriptures provide spiritual insight into the dynamic relationship between faithful financial stewardship and the overflow of divine blessings. They invite believers to participate actively in God's economy of generosity, reciprocity, and abundance.

Reflection and Application:

Consistency in Generosity: Reflecting on Malachi 3:10 and Luke 6:38 challenges believers to cultivate consistency in their generosity. The call to bring the whole tithe and the promise of overflowing blessings underscore the principle that God's generosity prompts and exceeds our own.

Trusting God's Reciprocal Blessings: Luke 6:38 encourages believers to trust in God's reciprocal blessings. As they give generously, they can anticipate God's response, which surpasses human expectations and reflects His abundant provision.

Active Participation in God's Economy: These passages call believers to actively participate in God's economy of generosity and reciprocity. It involves viewing financial stewardship as a partnership with God, trusting His promises, and eagerly anticipating the overflow of blessings that result from faithful honoring of God with wealth.

Seeking a Heart Transformation: Beyond financial transactions, these verses prompt a deeper reflection on the state of one's heart. Honoring God with wealth involves seeking a transformation of the heart, where generosity, gratitude, and trust become integral aspects of one's character.

As believers engage with the principles of honoring God with wealth, tithing faithfully, and embracing a reciprocal understanding of blessings, may they experience the transformative power of a generous and trusting heart, participating joyfully in God's economy of abundance.

3.2 Exploring the Concept of Tithing and Generosity in Biblical Context

This section delves deeper into the biblical context of tithing and generosity, exploring the historical and theological underpinnings of these practices. Tithing, a concept rooted in Old Testament teachings, and generosity, a timeless virtue emphasized throughout the Bible, provide a rich tapestry of principles that guide believers in their stewardship of resources.

Leviticus 27:30 - "A tithe of everything from the land, whether grain from the soil or fruit from the trees, belongs to the Lord; it is holy to the Lord."

The book of Leviticus outlines the principle of tithing, designating a tenth of all produce as belonging to the Lord. This practice was established to emphasize the sacredness of the first portion and to acknowledge God's ownership over the land and its abundance.

Malachi 3:10 - "Bring the whole tithe into the storehouse, that there may be food in my house. Test me in this," says the Lord Almighty, "and see if I will not throw open the floodgates of heaven and pour out so much blessing that there will not be room enough to store it."

Malachi reinforces the concept of tithing, urging believers to bring the whole tithe into God's house. The language of testing God in this matter highlights the reciprocal nature of the relationship, where faithful giving is met with overflowing blessings.

2 Corinthians 9:6-7 - "Remember this: Whoever sows sparingly will also reap sparingly, and whoever sows generously will also reap generously. Each of you should give what you have decided in your heart to give, not reluctantly or under compulsion, for God loves a cheerful giver."

In the New Testament, the Apostle Paul provides insights into the principles of generosity. The metaphor of sowing and reaping illustrates the proportional nature of blessings, emphasizing the joyous and voluntary nature of giving.

Practical Application:

Tithing as an Act of Worship: Leviticus 27:30 lays the foundation for tithing as an act of worship. By designating a portion of their resources to the Lord, believers express gratitude and acknowledge God's ownership and provision.

Testing God's Faithfulness: Malachi 3:10 invites believers to test God's faithfulness in the realm of tithing. It encourages stepping out in faith, trusting that God's promises of abundant blessings will manifest in response to faithful giving.

Generosity as a Lifestyle: 2 Corinthians 9:6-7 challenges believers to embrace generosity as a lifestyle. The emphasis on cheerful and voluntary giving reflects the transformative impact of a generous heart, where giving becomes an expression of joy and devotion.

Spiritual Insight:

Tithing and generosity are not mere financial transactions but spiritual practices that shape the character and disposition of the giver. They embody principles of trust, gratitude, and devotion to God.

Reflection and Application:

Reflecting on Tithing's Spiritual Significance: Leviticus 27:30 prompts believers to reflect on the spiritual significance of tithing. It encourages considering tithing not just as a financial obligation but as a sacred act that fosters a deeper connection with God.

Testing God's Promises: Malachi 3:10 challenges believers to test God's promises in the area of tithing. This reflection invites individuals to examine their faith and trust in God's provision, recognizing that faithful giving is met with God's abundant blessings.

Joyful and Voluntary Giving: 2 Corinthians 9:6-7 invites believers to assess their approach to giving. It encourages a shift from reluctant or obligatory giving to a joyful and voluntary disposition, recognizing that God values the attitude of the heart in generosity.

Balancing Old and New Testament Principles: As believers navigate the principles of tithing and generosity, there is an opportunity to understand the continuity of these principles across the Old and New Testaments. While the specific practices may differ, the underlying principles of worship, trust, and cheerful giving remain foundational.

As believers explore the concepts of tithing and generosity in their biblical context, may these principles inform and transform their financial stewardship, leading to a deeper understanding of God's provision and an enriched experience of the joy of giving.

- CHAPTER 4 -

The Dangers Of Love For Money

4.1 1 Timothy 6:10 - *"For the love of money is a root of all kinds of evil. Some people, eager for money, have wandered from the faith and pierced themselves with many griefs."*

This scripture from 1 Timothy 6:10 serves as a cautionary note, highlighting the potential dangers associated with the love of money. It underscores the need for a balanced and righteous perspective on wealth, recognizing the inherent risks of allowing financial pursuits to take precedence over spiritual well-being.

Interpreting 1 Timothy 6:10

The Love of Money as a Root: The verse identifies the love of money as a root of various kinds of evil. It implies that the excessive desire for wealth can lead to a variety of negative consequences, impacting not only individuals but also communities and societies.

Wandering from the Faith: The verse suggests that those who are eager for money may wander from their faith. The pursuit of wealth, when prioritized over spiritual values, can lead individuals away from their foundational beliefs and principles.

Self-Inflicted Griefs: The imagery of piercing oneself with many griefs conveys the self-inflicted nature of the troubles associated with the love of money. It implies that the consequences of prioritizing wealth can bring emotional, spiritual, and relational distress.

Practical Application:

Balancing Financial Goals with Faith: 1 Timothy 6:10 challenges believers to strike a balance between financial pursuits and their faith. It encourages them to assess their motivations for acquiring wealth and to prioritize spiritual well-being over the accumulation of riches.

Guarding Against Excessive Desire: The verse calls for self-reflection on one's desires for money. Believers are prompted to examine whether their eagerness for wealth is within the bounds of ethical and moral principles or if it has the potential to lead them down a harmful path.

Prioritizing Spiritual Values: Recognizing the risks associated with the love of money, believers are encouraged to prioritize spiritual values, integrity, and ethical conduct in their financial endeavors. This involves aligning financial decisions with a commitment to faith and moral principles.

Spiritual Insight:

1 Timothy 6:10 provides spiritual insight into the complex relationship between the pursuit of wealth and the potential erosion of spiritual foundations. It serves as a reminder that the love of money, when unchecked, can become a detrimental force that negatively impacts various aspects of an individual's life.

Reflection and Application:

Examining Motivations for Wealth: Believers are prompted to examine their motivations for seeking wealth. This involves a reflective assessment of whether financial pursuits align with ethical and spiritual principles or if they risk compromising foundational beliefs.

Cultivating Contentment: 1 Timothy 6:10 encourages a perspective of contentment. Rather than being driven by an insatiable desire for wealth, believers are urged to find satisfaction in their current circumstances, recognizing that true contentment transcends material possessions.

Seeking True Riches: The verse invites believers to redefine their understanding of riches. While financial prosperity is not inherently wrong, the caution lies in prioritizing "true riches"—those rooted in spiritual values, relational well-being, and a life aligned with God's principles.

Guarding Against the Deceptive Allure: Reflecting on this scripture serves as a safeguard against the deceptive allure of the love of money. It prompts believers to remain vigilant, recognizing the potential pitfalls and consequences associated with an unchecked desire for wealth.

Understanding the Context of 1 Timothy 6:10: The cautionary message in 1 Timothy 6:10 is part of Paul's instructions to Timothy regarding the challenges and responsibilities of leadership within the Christian community. It underscores the need for spiritual leaders and followers alike to maintain a proper perspective on wealth and avoid the pitfalls associated with its undue pursuit.

Cultural Relevance: In a contemporary context, where materialism and financial success are often emphasized, 1 Timothy 6:10 remains culturally relevant. It serves as a timeless reminder for individuals to assess their values and priorities in a society that can sometimes equate prosperity with personal worth.

Matthew 6:24 - "No one can serve two masters. Either you will hate the one and love the other, or you will be devoted to the one and despise the other. You cannot serve both God and money."

This verse from the Gospel of Matthew echoes the sentiment found in 1 Timothy 6:10 by highlighting the incompatibility of serving both God and money. It reinforces the notion that a divided loyalty between spiritual values and the pursuit of wealth can lead to inner conflict and moral compromise.

Practical Application:

Cultivating Spiritual Discernment: Matthew 6:24, when considered along-

Side 1 Timothy 6:10, emphasizes the importance of cultivating spiritual discernment. Believers are encouraged to evaluate their allegiances and ensure that their pursuit of financial goals aligns with their commitment to God.

Making Informed Financial Decisions: Both scriptures advocate for making informed and principled financial decisions. Believers are prompted to seek God's guidance in their financial endeavors, ensuring that their choices reflect a commitment to ethical conduct and spiritual values.

Promoting a Balanced Lifestyle: The combination of 1 Timothy 6:10 and Matthew 6:24 calls for a balanced lifestyle. It encourages believers to pursue financial goals responsibly while maintaining a primary allegiance to God, fostering a harmonious integration of faith and financial stewardship.

Spiritual Insight:

These scriptures provide spiritual insight into the interconnectedness of faith and finances. They highlight the profound impact that financial decisions can have on one's spiritual journey and underscore the need for intentional alignment with God's values in all aspects of life.

Reflection and Application:

Assessing Personal Allegiances: Reflecting on 1 Timothy 6:10 and Matthew 6:24 prompts believers to assess their personal allegiances. It encourages a thoughtful examination of whether their pursuit of wealth competes with their devotion to God and whether adjustments are needed to maintain a healthy balance.

Cultivating Financial Integrity: The combined wisdom of these scriptures encourages the cultivation of financial integrity. Believers are challenged to ensure that their financial pursuits are characterized by honesty, ethical decision-making, and a commitment to God's principles.

Seeking Contentment in God: In light of the potential pitfalls associated with the love of money, believers are encouraged to find true contentment in their relationship with God. The pursuit of a deeper connection with God can provide a sense of fulfillment that transcends material wealth.

Building a Kingdom-Oriented Perspective: Both scriptures invite believers to adopt a kingdom-oriented perspective in their financial decisions. It encourages a mindset where financial pursuits align with God's purposes, contributing to the advancement of His kingdom rather than self-centered accumulation.

As believers navigate the complex intersection of faith and finances, these scriptures provide guidance for maintaining a holistic and spiritually grounded approach. May the wisdom contained in 1 Timothy 6:10 and Matthew 6:24 inspire a commitment to financial stewardship that reflects the values of God's kingdom and fosters a life of integrity, contentment, and unwavering devotion to Him.

4.2 Understanding the Pitfalls of an Unhealthy Attachment to Wealth

This section delves deeper into the potential pitfalls associated with an unhealthy attachment to wealth, drawing insights from various scriptures that caution against the love of money. As believers seek a balanced perspective on finances, it is crucial to explore the potential dangers and consequences of allowing wealth to take precedence over spiritual well-being.

Ecclesiastes 5:10 - "Whoever loves money never has enough; whoever loves wealth is never satisfied with their income. This too is meaningless."

Ecclesiastes, often attributed to King Solomon, provides a poignant observation on the insatiable nature of the love of money. The pursuit of wealth, when driven by love for money itself, leads to perpetual dissatisfaction and a sense of meaninglessness.

Luke 12:15 - "Then he said to them, 'Watch out! Be on your guard against all kinds of greed; life does not consist in an abundance of possessions.'"

In the Gospel of Luke, Jesus issues a warning against all forms of greed, emphasizing that life's true essence is not found in the accumulation of possessions. This caution underscores the spiritual danger of allowing greed and an excessive desire for wealth to dictate one's priorities.

Practical Application:

Cultivating Contentment: Ecclesiastes 5:10 challenges believers to cultivate contentment, recognizing that the pursuit of wealth for its own sake is ultimately unsatisfying. It encourages an intentional shift toward finding meaning and fulfillment in a life centered on spiritual values rather than material abundance.

Guarding Against Greed: Luke 12:15 serves as a reminder to guard against greed in all its forms. Believers are prompted to assess their motivations and ensure that the pursuit of wealth aligns with a broader understanding of life's purpose, emphasizing relationships, service, and spiritual growth over material accumulation.

Proverbs 23:4-5 - "Do not wear yourself out to get rich; do not trust your own cleverness. Cast but a glance at riches, and they are gone, for they will surely sprout wings and fly off to the sky like an eagle."

The Book of Proverbs provides practical wisdom on the dangers of wearing oneself out in the relentless pursuit of wealth. The imagery of riches sprouting wings and flying away emphasizes the transient and unpredictable nature of material possessions.

Matthew 16:26 - "What good will it be for someone to gain the whole world, yet forfeit their soul? Or what can anyone give in exchange for their soul?"

In Matthew's Gospel, Jesus poses a rhetorical question that underscores the inherent value of one's soul over worldly gain. The pursuit of material wealth, if at the expense of spiritual well-being, is portrayed as a futile exchange with eternal consequences.

Spiritual Insight:

These scriptures offer spiritual insight into the potential dangers of an unhealthy attachment to wealth. They highlight the fleeting nature of material possessions and the profound consequences of prioritizing worldly gain over spiritual flourishing.

Reflection and Application:

Evaluating the Pursuit of Wealth: Reflecting on Ecclesiastes 5:10 and Proverbs 23:4-5 prompts believers to evaluate their approach to the pursuit of wealth. It encourages a measured and intentional pursuit that avoids excessive striving and acknowledges the impermanence of material possessions.

Prioritizing the Soul: Matthew 16:26 challenges believers to prioritize the well-being of their souls over worldly achievements. It prompts introspection on the true value of material possessions in light of eternity and encourages a shift toward a more balanced and spiritually grounded perspective.

Fostering an Eternal Perspective: Combining these scriptures encourages believers to foster an eternal perspective in their financial decisions. It involves recognizing the temporal nature of wealth and directing one's focus toward spiritual investments that have lasting significance.

Avoiding the Trap of Dissatisfaction: The cautionary messages in these scriptures serve as a warning against the trap of perpetual dissatisfaction that comes with an unhealthy attachment to wealth. Believers are encouraged to find contentment in their present circumstances, recognizing that true fulfillment goes beyond material abundance.

Understanding the Transience of Wealth: Proverbs 23:4-5 paints a vivid picture of the transience of wealth using the imagery of riches sprouting wings and flying away. This metaphor underscores the unpredictable nature of material possessions, reminding believers that reliance on wealth alone is an unstable foundation.

Weighing the Value of the Soul: Matthew 16:26 introduces a profound reflection on the value of the soul. It challenges believers to consider the eternal consequences of their pursuits, emphasizing that gaining the entire world is a hollow victory if it comes at the expense of forfeiting one's soul. This perspective encourages a recalibration of priorities toward spiritual well-being.

1 John 2:15-16 - "Do not love the world or anything in the world. If anyone loves the world, love for the Father is not in them. For everything in the world—the lust of the flesh, the lust of the eyes, and the pride of life—comes not from the Father but from the world."

In the first epistle of John, believers are cautioned against an unhealthy love for the world and its temporal pursuits. The lust of the flesh, the lust of the eyes, and the pride of life are identified as sources of temptation that can divert one's focus from the Father.

Practical Application:

Detaching from Worldly Desires: 1 John 2:15-16 challenges believers to detach from worldly desires that can lead to an unhealthy attachment to wealth. It prompts self-examination regarding the sources of motivation and encourages a redirection of focus toward spiritual values.

Embracing a Counter-Cultural Perspective: These scriptures call for an embrace of a counter-cultural perspective. In a world that often celebrates material success as the ultimate goal, believers are encouraged to adopt a mindset that values spiritual well-being, relational richness, and a life anchored in God's principles above all.

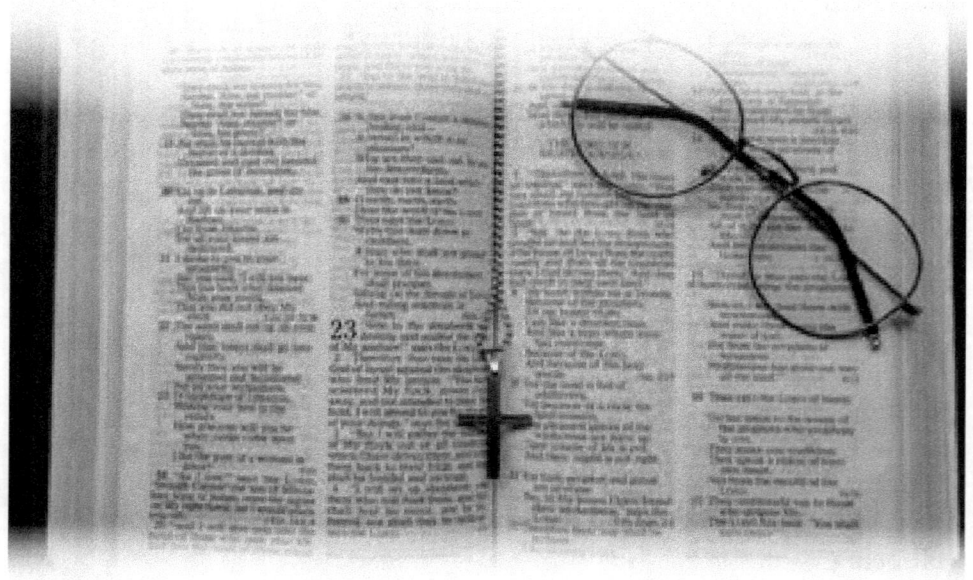

Spiritual Insight:

The combination of Proverbs 23:4-5, Matthew 16:26, and 1 John 2:15-16 provides spiritual insight into the multifaceted nature of an unhealthy attachment to wealth. It addresses not only the transience of material possessions but also the spiritual consequences of prioritizing worldly pursuits over the Father.

Reflection and Application:

Guarding Against Worldly Influences: Reflecting on these scriptures prompts believers to guard against the influences of the world that can foster an unhealthy attachment to wealth. It encourages intentional efforts to align priorities with God's values, resisting the allure of fleeting pleasures.

Developing a Kingdom-Centric Lifestyle: The wisdom found in Proverbs, Matthew, and 1 John inspires a shift toward a kingdom-centric lifestyle. Believers are encouraged to evaluate their choices, ensuring that their pursuits and attachments align with God's kingdom values rather than conforming to worldly standards.

Cultivating Spiritual Disciplines: In light of the potential pitfalls associated with an unhealthy attachment to wealth, these scriptures encourage believers to cultivate spiritual disciplines. This may include practices such as prayer, meditation on God's Word, and intentional efforts to foster a deeper relationship with God, providing a counterbalance to worldly influences.

Promoting a Culture of Contentment: The combined insights call for the promotion of a culture of contentment within the Christian community. By embracing the transient nature of wealth and prioritizing spiritual richness, believers can contribute to a community where fulfillment is sought in God rather than in material abundance.

As believers navigate the complexities of an ever-changing world, these scriptures guide them in understanding the pitfalls of an unhealthy attachment to wealth. May the wisdom contained in Proverbs 23:4-5, Matthew 16:26, and 1 John 2:15-16 inspire a deliberate and counter-cultural approach to financial stewardship, fostering a life marked by contentment, spiritual depth, and a steadfast commitment to the values of God's kingdom.

- CHAPTER 5 -

Contentment & Gratitude

5.1 Philippians 4:11-13 - *"I am not saying this because I am in need, for I have learned to be content whatever the circumstances. I know what it is to be in need, and I know what it is to have plenty. I have learned the secret of being content in any and every situation, whether well fed or hungry, whether living in plenty or in want."*

The passage from Philippians 4:11-13, expressed by the apostle Paul, reveals profound insights into the theme of contentment. In the midst of varying life circumstances, Paul shares the secret he has discovered—a contentment that transcends external conditions.

Interpreting Philippians 4:11-13

Learning Contentment: Paul declares that he has learned to be content in all circumstances, emphasizing that contentment is not an inherent trait but a cultivated skill. This implies an intentional and continuous process of understanding and embracing contentment, irrespective of external factors.

Experiencing Diverse Situations: Paul's acknowledgment of experiencing both need and plenty underscores the universality of the human experience. His encounters with varying circumstances serve as a testament to the applicability of contentment in all situations, regardless of their nature.

The Secret of Contentment: The passage unveils the secret of contentment, a lesson Paul has internalized through his journey. This secret is the ability to find satisfaction and peace, not in external conditions, but in a source that transcends circumstances.

Practical Application:

Cultivating a Contentment Mindset: Philippians 4:11-13 encourages believers to cultivate a mindset of contentment. It involves actively learning and practicing contentment, recognizing that it is not contingent on external factors but a state of the heart and mind.

Navigating Life's Extremes: The acknowledgment of experiencing both need and plenty resonates with believers navigating life's extremes. The passage prompts individuals to embrace contentment as a stabilizing force that remains unwavering amid the unpredictable ebbs and flows of life.

Discovering the Source of Content-

ment: The secret of contentment lies in discovering the source that transcends circumstances. For believers, this source is often found in a deep and trusting relationship with God, whose presence and promises provide a foundation for lasting contentment.

Spiritual Insight:

Philippians 4:11-13 offers spiritual insight into the transformative power of contentment. It reveals that contentment is not a passive acceptance of circumstances but an active and learned response rooted in a relationship with the divine.

Reflection and Application:

Reflecting on Personal Contentment: Believers are prompted to reflect on their own journey toward contentment. This involves acknowledging both areas of growth and areas that require further cultivation, recognizing that contentment is an ongoing process.

Embracing a Teachable Spirit: Paul's statement "I have learned" underscores the importance of a teachable spirit. Believers are encouraged to approach life with humility, openness to learning, and a willingness to be molded by the experiences that contribute to the cultivation of contentment.

Finding Contentment in God: The secret of contentment lies in finding satisfaction in God regardless of external circumstances. Believers are invited to deepen their relationship with God, allowing His presence and promises to become the anchor of their contentment amid life's fluctuations.

Applying Contentment Across Life's Spectrum: Philippians 4:11-13

challenges believers to apply contentment across the entire spectrum of life experiences—whether facing challenges or enjoying abundance. It encourages consistency in cultivating contentment as a resilient response to life's diverse situations.

As believers engage with the teachings of Philippians 4:11-13, may they find inspiration to pursue contentment as a learned and transformative aspect of their spiritual journey. May this passage guide them in embracing a contentment mindset that transcends external conditions, finding its ultimate source in a deep and abiding relationship with God.

Applying Contentment to Financial Stewardship:

Matthew 6:31-33 - *"So do not worry, saying, 'What shall we eat?' or 'What shall we drink?' or 'What shall we wear?' For the pagans run after all these things, and your heavenly Father knows that you need them. But seek first his kingdom and his righteousness, and all these things will be given to you as well."*

The teachings of Jesus in Matthew 6:31-33 complement the wisdom of Philippians 4:11-13 by addressing the common concerns related to material needs. Jesus encourages believers not to worry excessively about the necessities of life but rather to prioritize seeking God's kingdom and righteousness. This perspective aligns with the idea of cultivating contentment in reliance on God's provision.

Practical Application:

Prioritizing Kingdom Values: Matthew 6:31-33 encourages believers to prioritize seeking God's kingdom and righteousness over anxiously pursuing material needs. This application aligns with the essence of contentment found in Philippians, emphasizing a shift in focus from worldly concerns to spiritual priorities.

Trusting in God's Provision: Both passages underscore the importance of trusting in God's provision. Believers are encouraged to adopt an attitude of trust, recognizing that God knows their needs and is faithful to provide. This trust becomes a foundation for contentment in the face of life's uncertainties.

Spiritual Insight:

The combination of Philippians 4:11-13 and Matthew 6:31-33 provides spiritual insight into the interconnected nature of contentment and trust in God's provision. It emphasizes that contentment is not a passive resignation but an active reliance on God's faithfulness.

Reflection and Application:

Holistic Integration of Values: Believers are prompted to holistically integrate the values of contentment and trust in God's provision into their lives. This involves consciously aligning daily decisions, including financial stewardship, with the overarching pursuit of God's kingdom and righteousness.

Freedom from Excessive Worry: Reflecting on Matthew 6:31-33 in conjunction with Philippians 4:11-13 encourages believers to free themselves from excessive worry about material concerns. By prioritizing spiritual values, they can experience a profound sense of peace and contentment rooted in trust in God's loving care.

Balancing Ambition and Contentment: As individuals pursue their ambitions and goals, these scriptures guide them in striking a balance between ambition and contentment. It involves acknowledging desires and aspirations while maintaining a contented heart that trusts in God's timing and provision.

Seeking God in Financial Decision-Making: The teachings encourage believers to actively seek God in their financial decision-making processes. This involves prayerful consideration of how financial choices align with the principles of God's kingdom, righteousness, and the pursuit of contentment.

5.2 Finding True Riches in Contentment and Gratitude

Building upon the foundation of contentment explored in Philippians 4:11-13 and Matthew 6:31-33, this section delves into the spiritual principles of true riches found in a heart of contentment and gratitude. The combination of contentment and gratitude becomes a powerful force, reshaping perspectives on wealth and fostering a deeper connection with God.

Luke 12:15 - "Then he said to them, 'Watch out! Be on your guard against all kinds of greed; life does not consist in an abundance of possessions.'"

This warning from Jesus in Luke 12:15 reinforces the idea that life's true essence is not defined by material possessions. It serves as a caution against the relentless pursuit of abundance and highlights the need to find fulfillment beyond the accumulation of wealth.

Practical Application:

Guarding Against Greed: Luke 12:15 prompts believers to be vigilant against all forms of greed. This application reinforces the importance of cultivating contentment and gratitude, recognizing that life's richness is not solely determined by the abundance of possessions.

Shifting Perspectives on True Wealth: The verse encourages a shift in perspectives on true wealth. Believers are prompted to redefine the concept of richness, acknowledging that a life marked by contentment and gratitude holds a wealth that transcends material possessions.

Philippians 4:19 - "And my God will meet all your needs according to the riches of his glory in Christ Jesus."

The promise in Philippians 4:19 reinforces the idea that true riches come from God's abundant provision. It assures believers that their needs will be met according to the vast resources available in God's glory through Christ Jesus.

Practical Application:

Relying on God's Provision: Philippians 4:19 encourages believers to rely on God's provision rather than solely on their efforts or material accumulation. This application reinforces the connection between contentment and trust in God's ability to meet every need.

Shifting Dependency to Spiritual Riches: The promise in Philippians prompts a shift in dependency from worldly resources to spiritual riches. Believers are encouraged to prioritize their connection with God, recognizing that true abundance is found in the richness of a relationship with Him.

Spiritual Insight:

The combination of Luke 12:15 and Philippians 4:19 provides spiritual insight into the transformative power of contentment, gratitude, and reliance on God's provision. It unveils the path to true riches that goes beyond material possessions and leads to a fulfilling and spiritually enriched life.

Reflection and Application:

Cultivating a Grateful Heart: Believers are encouraged to cultivate a grateful heart as an integral part of contentment. This involves actively recognizing and appreciating the blessings in life, fostering an attitude of gratitude that contributes to a rich and fulfilling spiritual experience.

Embracing a Generous Spirit: True riches extend beyond personal gain. Reflecting on Luke 12:15 and Philippians 4:19 prompts believers to embrace a generous spirit, sharing the abundance of blessings with others and participating in God's work of provision in the lives of those in need.

Balancing Ambition with Gratitude: In the pursuit of goals and ambitions, these scriptures guide believers in balancing their drive for success with a heart of gratitude. It involves acknowledging achievements with thanksgiving and recognizing that true richness encompasses both material and spiritual blessings.

Chapter 6

Seeking God's Kingdom First

Building a Legacy of Contentment: The teachings encourage believers to build a legacy of contentment and gratitude. By modeling a life that values true riches, future generations can be inspired to prioritize a relationship with God over the pursuit of worldly possessions.

As believers incorporate the teachings from Luke 12:15 and Philippians 4:19 into their lives, may they find the true riches that come from a heart of contentment, gratitude, and reliance on God's provision. May this holistic perspective guide believers toward a life marked by spiritual fulfillment.

6.1 Matthew 6:33 - "But seek first his kingdom and his righteousness, and all these things will be given to you as well."

This pivotal verse from the Sermon on the Mount encapsulates Jesus' teachings on the priorities of life. Matthew 6:33 challenges believers to seek God's kingdom and righteousness as their foremost pursuit, assuring that God will provide for all their needs. This section explores the profound spiritual principles embedded in this verse.

Interpreting Matthew 6:33:

Seeking God's Kingdom: The directive to seek God's kingdom emphasizes prioritizing a relationship with God and aligning one's life with His purposes. It involves recognizing God's sovereignty and submitting to His lordship in every aspect of life.

Pursuing God's Righteousness: Seeking God's righteousness goes beyond mere moral conduct; it involves embracing a life in accordance with God's standards. This pursuit calls for a transformation of character, thought, and action to align with the principles of God's righteous kingdom.

The Promise of Provision: The assurance that "all these things will be given to you as well" underscores God's commitment to providing for the needs of those who prioritize His kingdom and righteousness. It establishes a divine partnership where material provisions are an outflow of spiritual alignment.

Practical Application:

Prioritizing Spiritual Values: Matthew 6:33 challenges believers to prioritize spiritual values over material concerns. This application involves intentional decision-making that places seeking God's kingdom and righteousness at the forefront of one's choices.

Aligning Life with God's Purposes: The verse prompts believers to evaluate whether their lives align with God's purposes. It involves an ongoing process of realignment, ensuring that daily decisions and actions are in harmony with the principles of God's righteous kingdom.

Spiritual Insight:

Matthew 6:33 provides spiritual insight into the inseparable connection between seeking God's kingdom and righteousness and experiencing divine provision. It unveils a profound truth—that true prosperity is found in a life devoted to God's purposes.

Reflection and Application:

Examining Priorities: Believers are encouraged to reflect on their priorities in light of Matthew 6:33. This involves an honest assessment of whether seeking God's kingdom and righteousness takes precedence over worldly pursuits and ambitions.

Understanding Divine Provision: The verse invites believers to deepen their understanding of divine provision. It challenges preconceived notions about material success and encourages a perspective that recognizes God as the ultimate provider, with material blessings flowing from a life centered on Him.

Integrating Faith and Finances: Matthew 6:33 calls for the integration of faith and finances. Believers are prompted to consider how their financial decisions align with the pursuit of God's kingdom and righteousness, recognizing that financial stewardship is a vital aspect of spiritual alignment.

Embracing a Kingdom-Centric Lifestyle: The teachings inspire believers to embrace a kingdom-centric lifestyle. This involves making choices that contribute to the advancement of God's kingdom on earth, recognizing that true prosperity is found in a life committed to His sovereign rule.

Navigating the Tension Between Spiritual Pursuits and Material Needs:

Matthew 6:34 - *"Therefore do not worry about tomorrow, for tomorrow will worry about itself. Each day has enough trouble of its own."*

Immediately following Matthew 6:33, Jesus addresses the natural concerns about the future. Matthew 6:34 encourages believers to live in the present moment, trusting God for daily needs and not allowing excessive worry about the future to overshadow their pursuit of His kingdom.

Practical Application:

Living in the Present Moment: Matthew 6:34 prompts believers to adopt a mindset of living in the present moment. This application involves releasing anxieties about the future and trusting God for each day's provision while maintaining a focus on seeking His kingdom and righteousness.

Balancing Prudence and Trust: While responsible planning is not discouraged, the verse encourages a balance between prudence and trust in God's providence. Believers are prompted to approach future uncertainties with a sense of trust, acknowledging that God is in control.

Spiritual Insight:

Matthew 6:34 provides spiritual insight into the delicate balance between practical living and spiritual trust. It emphasizes the importance of maintaining a steadfast focus on God's kingdom while addressing the natural concerns that arise in daily life.

Reflection and Application:

Assessing Anxiety and Trust: Believers are encouraged to assess their levels of anxiety and trust in God concerning the future. Reflecting on Matthew 6:34 prompts a consideration of whether worry is hindering the pursuit of God's kingdom and righteousness.

Embracing a Daily Dependence on God: The verse inspires believers to embrace a daily dependence on God. It challenges the notion of self-sufficiency and invites individuals to acknowledge their continual need for God's guidance, provision, and presence in their lives.

Applying Faith in Financial Planning: Matthew 6:34 encourages the integration of faith into financial planning. Believers are prompted to approach financial decisions with a sense of trust, acknowledging that God's sovereignty extends to all aspects of life, including financial well-being.

Finding Peace Amid Life's Challenges: The teachings guide believers in finding peace amid life's challenges. By focusing on seeking God's kingdom and righteousness and trusting God for each day, individuals can navigate difficulties with a sense of peace and assurance in God's faithfulness.

6.2 Prioritizing Spiritual Wealth and Trusting God's Provision

Building upon the teachings of Matthew 6:33 and 6:34, this section delves deeper into the principles of prioritizing spiritual wealth and trusting God's provision. The combination of seeking God's kingdom, living in the present moment, and trusting in divine provision forms a holistic approach to a life marked by true prosperity.

Proverbs 10:22 - "The blessing of the Lord brings wealth, without painful toil for it."

This proverbial wisdom encapsulates the idea that true wealth is a result of God's blessing rather than solely the product of human effort. It emphasizes the importance of aligning one's life with God's principles, which leads to a prosperity that transcends mere material accumulation.

Practical Application:

Embracing God's Blessing: Proverbs 10:22 encourages believers to embrace the concept of God's blessing as the source of true wealth. This application involves acknowledging the divine role in financial well-being and cultivating a life that invites God's favor.

Reevaluating the Pursuit of Wealth: The proverb prompts a reevaluation of the pursuit of wealth. Believers are encouraged to shift from a mindset of painful toil for material gain to a posture of seeking God's blessing through a life aligned with His kingdom and righteousness.

Spiritual Insight:

Proverbs 10:22 provides spiritual insight into the correlation between God's blessing and true wealth. It challenges conventional notions of prosperity and invites believers to recognize the spiritual dimensions of financial well-being.

Reflection and Application:

Assessing the Source of Prosperity: Believers are prompted to reflect on the source of their prosperity. Proverbs 10:22 encourages an evaluation of whether financial well-being is solely attributed to personal effort or if there is an acknowledgment of God's blessing.

Fostering a Blessing-Centric Lifestyle: The verse inspires a blessing-centric lifestyle. Believers are encouraged to actively cultivate an environment where God's favor and blessing are sought through a commitment to His kingdom, righteousness, and a trust in divine provision.

Aligning Values with Kingdom Principles: Proverbs 10:22 guides individuals in aligning their values with kingdom principles. It challenges the pursuit of wealth disconnected from God's blessing and encourages a reorientation towards a life marked by spiritual richness and divine favor.

Living in Gratitude for God's Provision: The teachings encourage believers to live in gratitude for God's provision. By recognizing God as the ultimate source of true wealth, individuals can approach their financial circumstances with a heart of thanksgiving and contentment.

As believers integrate the principles of Matthew 6:33, 6:34, and Proverbs 10:22 into their lives, may they experience a paradigm shift in their understanding of prosperity. May this holistic approach guide them toward prioritizing spiritual wealth, trusting in God's provision, and living a life marked by divine blessing. In doing so, may believers discover a deeper sense of purpose, contentment, and fulfillment that transcends the transient nature of material possessions.

Generosity as a Pathway to True Prosperity:

2 Corinthians 9:7 - *"Each of you should give what you have decided in your heart to give, not reluctantly or under compulsion, for God loves a cheerful giver."*

This verse from Paul's second letter to the Corinthians underscores the principle of generosity as a crucial aspect of true prosperity. It emphasizes the attitude with which giving should be approached—joyfully and willingly, as a response to God's love and provision.

Practical Application:

Cultivating a Joyful Giving Spirit: 2 Corinthians 9:7 encourages believers to cultivate a joyful and willing spirit of giving. This application involves approaching generosity as a joyful response to God's love and as an opportunity to contribute to His work in the world.

Aligning Giving with Heart Convictions: The verse prompts individuals to align their giving with the convictions of their hearts rather than external pressures. It encourages intentional and prayerful consideration of how financial resources can be used to further God's kingdom and bless others.

Spiritual Insight:

2 Corinthians 9:7 provides spiritual insight into the transformative power of generous giving. It highlights the relational aspect of giving, emphasizing the connection between a cheerful heart and the abundance of God's love.

Reflection and Application:

Evaluating the Motivation for Giving: Believers are encouraged to reflect on their motivations for giving. 2 Corinthians 9:7 prompts an examination of whether generosity is driven by a cheerful and willing heart or influenced by external expectations or obligations.

Integrating Generosity into Financial Stewardship: The verse inspires believers to integrate generosity into their overall financial stewardship. It challenges the compartmentalization of giving and encourages a seamless integration of financial decisions with the joy of contributing to God's work and the welfare of others.

Fostering a Culture of Joyful Giving: The teachings encourage the fostering of a culture of joyful giving within the Christian community. By embodying the principles of 2 Corinthians 9:7, believers contribute to a community marked by cheerful generosity, where giving becomes a celebration of God's provision and love.

Recognizing the Abundance of God's Provision: 2 Corinthians 9:7 invites believers to recognize the abundance of God's provision in their lives. It challenges a scarcity mindset and prompts individuals to view giving as an expression of gratitude for the overflowing blessings received from God.

As believers incorporate the principles of 2 Corinthians 9:7 into their financial practices, may they experience the liberating joy of generous giving. May this verse inspire a shift from reluctant or obligatory giving to a cheerful and willing spirit that aligns with God's abundant love and provision. In doing so, may believers discover a pathway to true prosperity that goes beyond material wealth and encompasses the richness of a generous and joyful heart.

Prioritizing Spiritual Wealth and Trusting God's Provision

Building upon the teachings of Matthew 6:33 and 6:34, this section delves deeper into the principles of prioritizing spiritual wealth and trusting God's provision. The combination of seeking God's kingdom, living in the present moment, and trusting in divine provision forms a holistic approach to a life marked by true prosperity.

Proverbs 10:22 - "The blessing of the Lord brings wealth, without painful toil for it."

This proverbial wisdom encapsulates the idea that true wealth is a result of God's blessing rather than solely the product of human effort. It emphasizes the importance of aligning one's life with God's principles, which leads to a prosperity that transcends mere material accumulation.

Practical Application:

Embracing God's Blessing: Proverbs 10:22 encourages believers to embrace the concept of God's blessing as the source of true wealth. This application involves acknowledging the divine role in financial well-being and cultivating a life that invites God's favor.

Reevaluating the Pursuit of Wealth: The proverb prompts a reevaluation of the pursuit of wealth. Believers are encouraged to shift from a mindset of painful toil for material gain to a posture of seeking God's blessing through a life aligned with His kingdom and righteousness.

Spiritual Insight:

Proverbs 10:22 provides spiritual insight into the correlation between God's blessing and true wealth. It challenges conventional notions of prosperity and invites believers to recognize the spiritual dimensions of financial well-being.

Reflection and Application:

Assessing the Source of Prosperity: Believers are prompted to reflect on the source of their prosperity. Proverbs 10:22 encourages an evaluation of whether financial well-being is solely attributed to personal effort or if there is an acknowledgment of God's blessing.

Fostering a Blessing-Centric Lifestyle: The verse inspires a blessing-centric lifestyle. Believers are encouraged to actively cultivate an environment where God's favor and blessing are sought through a commitment to His kingdom, righteousness, and a trust in divine provision.

Aligning Values with Kingdom Principles: Proverbs 10:22 guides individuals in aligning their values with kingdom principles. It challenges the pursuit of wealth disconnected from God's blessing and encourages a reorientation towards a life marked by spiritual richness and divine favor.

Living in Gratitude for God's Provision: The teachings encourage believers to live in gratitude for God's provision. By recognizing God as the ultimate source of true wealth, individuals can approach their financial circumstances with a heart of thanksgiving and contentment.

As believers integrate the principles of Matthew 6:33, 6:34, and Proverbs 10:22 into their lives, may they experience a paradigm shift in their understanding of prosperity. May this holistic approach guide them toward prioritizing spiritual wealth, trusting in God's provision, and living a life marked by divine blessing. In doing so, may believers discover a deeper sense of purpose, contentment, and fulfillment that transcends the transient nature of material possessions.

- CHAPTER 7 -

Investing in Eternal Treasures

7.1 Matthew 6:19-21 - *"Do not store up for yourselves treasures on earth, where moths and vermin destroy, and where thieves break in and steal. But store up for yourselves treasures in heaven, where moths and vermin do not destroy, and where thieves do not break in and steal. For where your treasure is, there your heart will be also."*

This passage from the Sermon on the Mount presents Jesus' profound teachings on the nature of treasures. It calls believers to shift their focus from earthly possessions, which are susceptible to decay and theft, to heavenly treasures that endure for eternity. This section explores the spiritual principles embedded in these verses.

Interpreting Matthew 6:19-21

Earthly vs. Heavenly Treasures: The passage contrasts the temporal nature of earthly treasures, susceptible to decay and theft, with the enduring nature of treasures stored in heaven. It challenges believers to reconsider their priorities and investments, recognizing the fleeting nature of worldly possessions.

The Connection Between Treasure and Heart: The verses establish a profound connection between one's treasure and the orientation of the heart.

The location of a person's treasure—whether on earth or in heaven—reveals the true focus and allegiance of their heart.

Practical Application:

Reevaluating Material Attachments: Matthew 6:19-21 prompts believers to reevaluate their attachments to material possessions. This application involves a conscious examination of whether the pursuit of earthly treasures has become a focal point in their lives.

Investing in Eternal Significance: The passage encourages believers to redirect their investments towards eternal significance. This application involves intentional choices that contribute to the advancement of God's kingdom, the well-being of others, and the storing up of treasures in heaven.

Spiritual Insight:

Matthew 6:19-21 provides spiritual insight into the transformative power of aligning one's treasures with heavenly values. It underscores the intimate connection between the orientation of the heart and the location of one's treasure.

Reflection and Application:

Examining the Impact of Materialism: Believers are encouraged to reflect on the impact of materialism in their lives. Matthew 6:19-21 prompts an examination of whether the pursuit of earthly treasures has influenced their priorities, decisions, and overall sense of contentment.

Prioritizing Eternal Investments: The verses inspire believers to prioritize investments with eternal significance. This involves intentional choices in how time, resources, and talents are utilized, with a focus on contributing to the kingdom of God and the well-being of others.

Cultivating a Heavenly Perspective: The teachings guide believers in cultivating a heavenly perspective on wealth. By recognizing the transient nature of earthly treasures, individuals can shift their focus to investments that align with God's values and contribute to the eternal realm.

Aligning the Heart with God's Priorities: Matthew 6:19-21 encourages believers to align their hearts with God's priorities. As they invest in heavenly treasures, their hearts become attuned to the values of God's kingdom, fostering a sense of purpose, fulfillment, and an enduring legacy.

As believers incorporate the teachings of Matthew 6:19-21 into their lives, may they experience a transformative shift in their perspectives on wealth. May this passage inspire a redirection of investments towards eternal significance, cultivating a heavenly perspective that shapes priorities and fosters a deep alignment with the values of God's kingdom. In doing so, may believers find true treasures that endure beyond the transient nature of earthly possessions.

7.2 The Principle of Single-minded Devotion:

Matthew 6:22-24 - "The eye is the lamp of the body. If your eyes are healthy, your whole body will be full of light. But if your eyes are unhealthy, your whole body will be full of darkness. If then the light within you is darkness, how great is that darkness! No one can serve two masters. Either you will hate the one and love the other, or you will be devoted to the one and despise the other. You cannot serve both God and money."

This continuation of Jesus' teachings further emphasizes the principle of single-minded devotion. The metaphor of the eye as the lamp of the body underscores the importance of maintaining spiritual clarity and focus. The passage concludes with a powerful declaration about the impossibility of serving both God and money.

Interpreting Matthew 6:22-24

The Healthy Eye: A healthy eye symbolizes spiritual clarity and a focused devotion to God. It represents a life characterized by righteousness, wisdom, and a singular pursuit of God's kingdom.

The Unhealthy Eye: An unhealthy eye signifies a lack of spiritual focus, leading to darkness within. It represents a divided heart, wavering between loyalty to God and the pursuit of worldly wealth.

The Incompatibility of Serving Two Masters: Jesus unequivocally states that serving both God and money is impossible. This declaration highlights the need for a
singular, undivided allegiance in matters of devotion and
priorities.

Practical Application:

Cultivating Spiritual Clarity: Matthew 6:22 encourages believers to cultivate spiritual clarity, symbolized by a healthy eye. This involves maintaining a focus on God's kingdom values and aligning one's vision with heavenly priorities.

Guarding Against Divided
Allegiance: The passage prompts believers to guard against a divided allegiance. It challenges them to examine their hearts and ensure that their devotion is undivided, with God as the sole master of their lives.

Spiritual Insight:

Matthew 6:22-24 provides spiritual insight into the profound connection between spiritual focus, undivided allegiance, and the pursuit of God's kingdom. It underscores the transformative power of maintaining a healthy eye in the spiritual journey.

Reflection and Application:

Evaluating Spiritual Focus: Believers are encouraged to reflect on their spiritual focus. Matthew 6:22 prompts an evaluation of whether their eyes are healthy, radiating spiritual clarity, or if there is a need for realignment towards God's kingdom.

Assessing Allegiance: The passage inspires believers to assess their allegiance. It challenges individuals to examine whether they are serving God wholeheartedly or if there is a compromise in their devotion due to the pursuit of material wealth.

Choosing Singular Devotion: Matthew 6:24 guides believers in making a conscious choice of singular devotion. It calls for a decision to prioritize God above all else, recognizing the incompatibility of serving both God and money.

Guarding Against Spiritual Darkness: The teachings warn against spiritual darkness resulting from divided allegiance. Believers are prompted to guard against any compromise that may obscure the light of God's truth within them.

Understanding the Impermanence of Earthly Wealth and the Importance of Eternal Investments

Building upon the teachings of Matthew 6:19-21 and 6:22-24, this section explores the impermanence of earthly wealth and the profound importance of making eternal investments. The combination of these principles offers a comprehensive perspective on wealth, urging believers to focus on what truly endures.

Ecclesiastes 5:10 - "Whoever loves money never has enough; whoever loves wealth is never satisfied with their income. This too is meaningless."

This verse from Ecclesiastes highlights the insatiable nature of a love for money and wealth. It echoes the sentiments expressed by Jesus in Matthew, emphasizing the futility of finding lasting satisfaction in the pursuit of material abundance.

Interpreting Ecclesiastes 5:10

The Endless Quest for Wealth: The verse exposes the never-ending quest for wealth that characterizes those who love money. It serves as a cautionary reminder of the inherent dissatisfaction associated with a relentless pursuit of material abundance.
Practical Application:

Cultivating Contentment: Ecclesiastes 5:10 encourages believers to cultivate contentment. This application involves recognizing the limitations of wealth in providing lasting satisfaction and finding fulfillment in a life anchored in spiritual values.

Balancing Ambition and Gratitude: The verse prompts believers to balance their ambitions with gratitude for what they have. It challenges the mindset that constantly seeks more and encourages an appreciation for the blessings already present in their lives.

Spiritual Insight:

Ecclesiastes 5:10 provides spiritual insight into the deceptive allure of wealth and the perpetual dissatisfaction that accompanies an obsessive pursuit of material abundance. It calls for a shift in focus from accumulating wealth to finding contentment in a life centered on eternal values.

Reflection and Application:

Reflecting on Personal Ambitions: Believers are encouraged to reflect on their personal ambitions, especially those related to financial success. Ecclesiastes 5:10 prompts an examination of whether the pursuit of wealth has become a primary driving force in their lives.

Acknowledging the Limitations of Wealth: The verse invites believers to acknowledge the limitations of wealth in providing lasting satisfaction. It encourages a realistic assessment of whether the pursuit of material abundance has brought the anticipated fulfillment.

Choosing Contentment in Spiritual Values: Ecclesiastes 5:10 guides individuals in choosing contentment in spiritual values rather than relying on the accumulation of wealth for satisfaction. It challenges believers to find true meaning and purpose in a life anchored in eternal investments.

Embracing a Grateful Heart: The teachings inspire believers to embrace a grateful heart. Ecclesiastes 5:10 encourages an attitude of thankfulness for the blessings present in their lives, fostering contentment and redirecting focus towards spiritual richness.

As believers integrate the teachings of Ecclesiastes 5:10 into their lives, may they experience a transformative shift in their perspectives on wealth. May this verse serve as a reminder of the impermanence of earthly pursuits and the importance of finding lasting satisfaction in eternal investments. In doing so, may believers cultivate contentment, balance ambition with gratitude, and discover true prosperity in a life anchored in spiritual values.

- CHAPTER 8 -

Conclusion

8.1 Recapitulation of Key Biblical Principles on Money and Wealth

As we conclude this journey through biblical teachings on money and wealth, let's reflect on the key principles we've explored. The wisdom from various scriptures offers profound insights into the proper perspective and use of financial resources.

1. Prioritizing God's Kingdom (Matthew 6:33)

Principle: Seek first God's kingdom and righteousness, and trust that He will provide for your needs.

Application: Prioritize spiritual values over material concerns and align daily decisions with God's purposes.

2. Stewardship and Generosity (2 Corinthians 9:7)

Principle: God loves a cheerful giver; give willingly and joyfully from the heart.

Application: Cultivate a spirit of generosity, align financial decisions with God's will, and contribute to the well-being of others.

3. Treasures in Heaven (Matthew 6:19-21)

Principle: Store up treasures in heaven, for where your treasure is, there your heart will be also.

Application: Redirect investments towards eternal significance, recognizing the impermanence of earthly possessions.

4. Single-minded Devotion (Matthew 6:22-24):

Principle: Maintain a healthy eye, serving God wholeheartedly without divided allegiance to money.

Application: Cultivate spiritual clarity, guard against divided loyalties, and make a conscious choice for singular devotion to God.

5. Impermanence of Earthly Wealth (Ecclesiastes 5:10)

Principle: The love of money is insatiable, and wealth alone does not bring lasting satisfaction.

Application: Cultivate contentment, balance ambitions with gratitude, and find fulfillment in spiritual values rather than relentless pursuit of material abundance.

Recapitulation Reflection:

As we reflect on these principles, it becomes clear that biblical teachings on money and wealth are not just about financial management but encompass a holistic approach to life. They guide believers to prioritize spiritual values, embrace generosity, invest in eternal significance, maintain undivided devotion, and find contentment beyond material pursuits.

May these biblical principles serve as a guide in navigating the complexities of financial stewardship, leading to a life marked by spiritual fulfillment, generosity, and a profound connection with God's purposes. In embracing these principles, believers can discover true prosperity that extends beyond the transient nature of earthly possessions, finding lasting meaning and purpose in their journey of faith.

6. Tithing and Firstfruits (Proverbs 3:9-10)

Principle: Honor the Lord with your wealth and the firstfruits of your crops, and in return, your barns will be filled to overflowing.

Application: Embrace the practice of tithing and giving the first portion of your income to God, recognizing Him as the ultimate source of your prosperity.

7. Caution Against the Love of Money (1 Timothy 6:10)

Principle: The love of money is a root of all kinds of evil, leading some to wander from the faith and experience many griefs.

Application: Be mindful of the potential dangers associated with an excessive attachment to wealth and prioritize a healthy relationship with money to avoid negative spiritual consequences.

8. Contentment in All Circumstances (Philippians 4:11-13)

Principle: True contentment is found in being content in all circumstances, whether in need or in plenty, through Christ's strength.

Application: Cultivate a spirit of contentment, recognizing that true riches come from a relationship with Christ and not solely from material abundance.

9. Seeking God's Kingdom First (Matthew 6:33 - Recapitulation)

Principle: Seek first God's kingdom and righteousness, trusting that God will provide for all your needs.

Application: Continually prioritize God's kingdom in all areas of life, recognizing that spiritual pursuits take precedence over material concerns. Recapitulation Reflection:

The additional principles highlight the importance of consistent giving through tithing, cautioning against the potential pitfalls of an unhealthy attachment to money, and emphasizing contentment in every circumstance. Together with the previously discussed principles, these teachings offer a comprehensive framework for financial stewardship, encouraging believers to approach wealth with a heart aligned with God's values.

As believers reflect on these principles collectively, they are equipped with a rich foundation for navigating the complexities of financial decisions. May these biblical teachings guide individuals toward a holistic and spiritually enriching approach to money and wealth, fostering a deeper connection with God and a life marked by true prosperity.

9.2 Encouragement for a Balanced and God-Centered Approach to Finances

As we conclude our exploration of biblical principles on money and wealth, let's delve into words of encouragement and practical guidance for maintaining a balanced and God-centered approach to finances.

1. The Joy of Generosity (Acts 20:35)

Encouragement: "It is more blessed to give than to receive."

Guidance: Find joy in generous giving, understanding that the act of giving brings greater blessings than receiving. Generosity aligns your heart with God's character and fosters a sense of fulfillment.

2. Financial Wisdom through Prayer (James 1:5)

Encouragement: "If any of you lacks wisdom, you should ask God, who gives generously to all without finding fault, and it will be given to you."

Guidance: Approach financial decisions with prayer, seeking God's wisdom in managing resources, making investments, and navigating financial challenges. Trust in God's generous provision and guidance.

3. Trusting God in Times of Need (Philippians 4:19)

Encouragement: "And my God will meet all your needs according to the riches of his glory in Christ Jesus."

Guidance: Trust that God will provide for your needs, even in challenging times. Rely on His abundance and faithfulness, recognizing that He is the ultimate source of provision.

4. Gratitude in Abundance and Scarcity (1 Thessalonians 5:18)

Encouragement: "Give thanks in all circumstances; for this is God's will for you in Christ Jesus."

Guidance: Cultivate a heart of gratitude regardless of financial circumstances. Whether in abundance or scarcity, express thankfulness for God's provision and trust in His divine plan.

5. Seeking God's Guidance in Financial Planning (Proverbs 16:3)

Encouragement: "Commit to the Lord whatever you do, and he will establish your plans."

Guidance: Involve God in your financial planning and decision-making. Commit your plans to Him, seeking His guidance and trusting that He will establish your path according to His will.

6. The Importance of Financial Accountability (Proverbs 27:23)

Encouragement: "Be sure you know the condition of your flocks, give careful attention to your herds."

Guidance: Be proactive in managing your finances. Understand your financial situation, budget wisely, and be accountable for your resources. Responsible stewardship is a reflection of your commitment to God's principles.

7. The Blessing of Contentment (1 Timothy 6:6-8)

Encouragement: "But godliness with contentment is great gain. For we brought nothing into the world, and we can take nothing out of it. But if we have food and clothing, we will be content with that."

Guidance: Find contentment in godliness rather than the pursuit of material possessions. Recognize that true gain lies in a heart content with the basics of life, understanding that material wealth is temporary.

8. Planning for the Future with God (Proverbs 21:5)

Encouragement: "The plans of the diligent lead to profit as surely as haste leads to poverty."

Guidance: Approach financial planning with diligence and patience. Trust that God honors thoughtful and well-executed plans. Consider the future with wisdom, keeping God at the center of your financial decisions.

9. Wise Counsel in Financial Matters (Proverbs 15:22)

Encouragement: "Plans fail for lack of counsel, but with many advisers, they succeed."

Guidance: Seek wise counsel in financial matters. Surround yourself with mentors, financial advisors, and fellow believers who can provide guidance and accountability. Make decisions with collective wisdom.

10. Understanding the Source of True Riches (Luke 12:15)

Encouragement: "Then he said to them, 'Watch out! Be on your guard against all kinds of greed; life does not consist in an abundance of possessions.'"

Guidance: Guard against greed and the illusion that life's meaning is found in material possessions. Understand that true richness is found in a relationship with God, living a life of purpose, and contributing to the well-being of others.

11. A Heart of Thankfulness (Colossians 3:15)

Encouragement: "Let the peace of Christ rule in your hearts, since as members of one body you were called to peace. And be thankful."

Guidance: Allow the peace of Christ to rule in your heart, fostering a spirit of gratitude. Approach financial decisions with a thankful heart, recognizing the blessings of God in both financial abundance and challenges.

Encouragement Reflection:

In these additional encouragements, believers are reminded of the blessing found in contentment, the importance of diligent planning for the future, the value of wise counsel, the understanding of true riches, and the cultivation of a heart filled with thankfulness.

May these encouragements serve as a source of inspiration for individuals striving to maintain a balanced and God-centered approach to finances. By incorporating these principles into their lives, believers can experience a deep sense of contentment, wisdom in planning, and a heart overflowing with gratitude, ultimately fostering a life marked by financial stewardship aligned with God's purposes.

www.ingramcontent.com/pod-product-compliance
Lightning Source LLC
Chambersburg PA
CBHW070354230526
45471CB00006B/2560